Earthquakes

WITNESS TO DISASTER

"It is amazing how the Earth tells us that it is alive, that it moves and changes like any living organism."

Dr. Alberto M. Lopez-Venegas,
United States Geological Survey

Running about 800 miles (1,300 km) along California's Pacific coast, and about 10 miles (16 km) deep, the San Andreas Fault marks the boundary between the North American Plate and the Pacific plate. This photograph was taken with a fisheye lens, which exaggerates the curve of the Earth.

Earthquakes

WITNESS TO DISASTER

JUDY & DENNIS FRADIN

NATIONAL GEOGRAPHIC

WASHINGTON, D.C.

Text copyright © 2008 Judith Bloom Fradin and Dennis Brindell Fradin

Founded in 1888, the National Geographic Society is one of the largest nonprofit scientific and educational organizations in the world. It reaches more than 285 million people worldwide each month through its official journal, NATIONAL GEOGRAPHIC, and its four other magazines; the National Geographic Channel; television documentaries; radio programs; films; books; videos and DVDs; maps; and interactive media. National Geographic has funded more than 8,000 scientific research projects and supports an education program combating geographic illiteracy.

For more information, please call 1-800-NGS-LINE (647-5463) or write to the following address:
National Geographic Society
1145 17th Street N.W.
Washington, D.C. 20036-4688
U.S.A.

Visit us online at www.nationalgeographic.com/books

For information about special discounts for bulk purchases, please contact National Geographic Books Special Sales at ngspecsales@ngs.org

For rights or permissions inquiries, please contact National Geographic Books Subsidiary Rights: ngbookrights@ngs.org

Fradin, Judith Bloom.
  Earthquakes : witness to disaster / by Judy and Dennis Fradin.
    p. cm. — (Witness to disaster)
Includes bibliographical references.
ISBN 978-1-4263-0211-4 (hardcover)
ISBN 978-1-4263-0212-1 (lib. bdg.)
1. Earthquakes — Alaska — Anchorage region. I. Fradin, Judith Bloom. II. Fradin, Dennis B. III. Title.
QE535.2.U6F68 2008
551.22 — dc22
                                    2007044164

Hardcover ISBN: 978-1-4263-0211-4
Library Edition ISBN: 978-1-4263-0212-1
Printed in China

Series design by Daniel Banks, Project Design Company; Designer, Kerri Sarembock, Project Design Company

National Geographic Society
John M. Fahey, Jr., President and Chief Executive Officer;
Gilbert M. Grosvenor, Chairman of the Board;
Tim T. Kelly, President, Global Media Group;
Nina D. Hoffman, Executive Vice President; President, Books Publishing Group

Staff for This Book
Nancy Laties Feresten, Vice President, Editor-in-Chief of Children's Books
Amy Shields, Executive Editor
Bea Jackson, Director of Design and Illustration
Jim Hiscott, Art Director
Lori Epstein, Illustrations Editor
Jean Cantu, Illustrations Specialist
Carl Mehler, Director of Maps
Jennifer A. Thornton, Managing Editor
Priyanka Lamichhane, Assistant Editor
R. Gary Colbert, Production Director
Lewis R. Bassford, Production Manager
Maryclare Tracy, Nicole Elliott, Manufacturing Managers

Photo Credits
cover, Reza / NG Image Collection; back, Emory Kristof / NG Image Collection; spine, Bill Roth/ Anchorage Daily News/ Associated Press; 2-3, James Balog/Getty Images; 5, Koji Sasahara/ Associated Press; 6, Ward W. Wells/ Anchorage Museum at Rasmuson Center; 9, Pratt Museum; 10, Stan Wayman/Life Magazine, Copyright Time Inc./Time Life Pictures/Getty Images; 11, Central Press/Getty Images; 12, Chiaki Tsukumo/ Associated Press; 13, Museum of Fine Arts, Boston. Reproduced with permission. c2000 Museum of Fine Arts, Boston. All Rights Reserved; 15, NG Image Collection; 16 up left, Susan Sanford/ NG Image Collection; 16 up right, Susan Sanford / NG Image Collection; 16 lo left, Susan Sanford / NG Image Collection; 16 lo right, Susan Sanford / NG Image Collection; 18, Ann Johansson/ Associated Press; 19, Kashuhiro Nogi/ AFP/ Getty Images; 21, J.R. Stacy/ USGS; 22, Library of Congress; 23, National Information Service for Earthquake Engineering, EERC, University of California, Berkeley; 25, USGS; 26, Newspaperarchive.com; 27, Library of Congress; 28, J. B. Macelwane Archives, Saint Louis University; 29, USGS; 31, T. Kuribayashi, National Information Service for Earthquake Engineering, EERC, University of California, Berkeley; 32, Chris Sattlberger/ Photo Researchers, Inc.; 33, Banaras Khan/ AFP/ Getty Images; 35, Mike Poland/ USGS; 37, Commander Emily B. Christman/ NOAA; 38, Chuck Nacke//Time Life Pictures/Getty Images; 39, C.E. Meyer/ USGS; 40-41, Farzaneh Khademian/Corbis; 42, Jim Holmes/ Axiom/ Getty Images; 43, Reza / NG Image Collection; 44, Keystone/ Getty Images;

CONTENTS

CHAPTER 1

"The Ground Would Not Stop Shaking"
Alaska, 1964

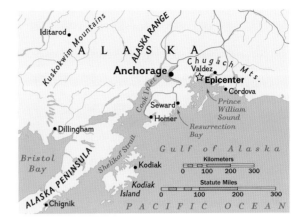

The afternoon of March 27, 1964, seemed to be shaping up as a pleasant time for thousands of Alaskans. In Anchorage and other cities, people were heading home from work, preparing dinner, or getting ready for Easter weekend. But then something happened to make that Good Friday a day that Alaskans will never forget. At 5:36 p.m., 13 miles below ground in southern Alaska, massive blocks of rock suddenly shifted and snapped, causing a gigantic earthquake.

"I was next door at my friend Raymond's house when it started," Michele Doran recalls about that afternoon. Along with nearly 50,000 other people, eight-year-old Michele lived in Anchorage, Alaska's biggest city. "We were watching cartoons and dancing. We had experienced lots of small quakes before, so at first we weren't scared."

The shaking quickly intensified. "It got a *lot* worse," says Michele. "The TV fell and broke. Soon the house was tipping. I couldn't stand up to get out of the house. I had to crawl on my hands and knees. Then I couldn't even move but could only lie flat on the floor.

> "I turned and watched my house squirm and groan, as though in last mortal agony. It was as though someone had engaged it in a gigantic taffy pull, stretching it, shrinking it, and twisting it."

Robert B. Atwood, then editor and publisher of the *Anchorage Daily Times*

One half of 4th Avenue in downtown Anchorage, Alaska—stores and all—dropped six to eight feet below street level after the quake.

"You know that really loud sound when a jet airplane slows down and reverses its engines? That's what the earthquake sounded like."

Michele Doran, who was eight years old and living with her family in Anchorage, Alaska, at the time of the quake

"It came in waves. It would ease up a little, then there'd be a terrible, loud, rolling sound which meant that the really bad shaking was starting again. It happened over and over and over: the loud sound, then the shaking."

Three hundred miles away in the town of Old Harbor, on Kodiak Island, Viola Simeonoff was having a similar experience. She was at her friend Rundina's house. "Rundina's older sister told us we had to get out of the house, but I couldn't move because the floor was moving funny. Finally I got outside. The ground would not stop shaking—it went on it seemed like forever. When I looked up at the nearby mountainsides, the snow was coming off of them, like giant snowballs rolling down. When it finally stopped, Rundina's dad told me to go home, that lots of water would be coming."

During the five minutes it lasted, the quake caused enormous damage across 50,000 square miles of Alaska. Giant cracks split the ground. *Landslides* and avalanches hurled huge amounts of dirt, rocks, ice, and snow down mountain slopes. Buildings swayed and fell. Railroad tracks twisted. Bridges collapsed. Cars bounced up and down as if on trampolines. Twenty people lost their lives. Three-quarters of the city of Anchorage was damaged or destroyed.

But the Good Friday Earthquake held another danger. As the father of Viola's friend warned, lots of water would be coming.

Earthquakes that originate beneath or near the ocean can disturb the water, creating *tsunamis*. These waves, which travel at speeds of more than 500 miles per hour, are not very tall when out at sea. As they approach shore, however, tsunamis pile up into giant walls of water that flatten everything in their path.

WITNESS TO A TSUNAMI

"Dad was the last one to get up on the roof. Just as he did, the wave hit. It was enormous. The wave destroyed everything in the neighborhood except the house we were on. It was ripped off the foundation and we were sent spinning around in the water as we hung on to the roof shingles. I felt like I was in the house in The Wizard of Oz. *I saw our car float by. We swirled around in the water for 15 or 20 minutes until the house got stuck in some trees about a mile from where we started."*

Linda McRae MacSwain, then 15 years old, recalling how she and her family survived the tsunamis on a rooftop in Seward, Alaska

LIFE

In Color: EARTHQUAKE IN ALASKA

The destruction of Turnagain Heights, an Anchorage neighborhood built on a bluff that collapsed, made the cover of *LIFE*, a popular magazine known for its photographs.

Alaska's Good Friday Earthquake, which originated near an ocean inlet named Prince William Sound, generated huge tsunamis. A few minutes after the quake, one tsunami approached Valdez, Alaska. The 30-foot wave ripped away a dock and drowned 28 people before destroying much of the town.

At about the same time, a 70-foot wave struck Chenega, a Native-Alaskan community on an island in Prince William Sound. Twenty-three of the village's 76 residents drowned.

Fishing boats were carried inland five blocks or more by the tsunami that followed the Good Friday quake.

Twenty minutes after the quake, a 40-foot-high tsunami slammed into Seward. It was followed by five more waves over the next few hours. Tsunamis barraged the town of Kodiak roughly once an hour until 3 a.m. Most of downtown Kodiak was destroyed. When contacted by radio, one captain reported that his fishing boat had landed safely—five blocks from shore behind a schoolhouse.

At Old Harbor, town leaders knew that tsunamis would follow such a strong quake, and they directed people to high ground. Many of Old Harbor's 200 residents, including Viola Simeonoff, spent the night on a hill. "All night, we heard wave after wave banging against the houses below," she says. "In the morning I saw that the water had destroyed our whole town."

Tsunamis created by the quake traveled far beyond Alaska. In the middle of the night, four slammed into Crescent City, California, 1,700 miles from Anchorage.

In all, Alaska's Good Friday Earthquake took approximately 132 lives—most of them in the tsunamis. Besides the human loss, $750 million in property (equal to $4.5 billion today) was destroyed by the most powerful North American earthquake ever recorded.

CHAPTER 2

"As If a Giant Foot Had Stepped On It"

Why Does the Earth Quake?

The January 17, 1995, earthquake in Kobe, Japan, toppled the elevated Hanshin Expressway.

Since ancient times, people have wondered: Why does the ground sometimes shake?

The ancient Greeks believed that their god Atlas lost a war against Zeus, the king of the gods. Zeus condemned Atlas to bear the Earth on his shoulders. To ease this burden, Atlas sometimes shifted the world from one shoulder to the other. When he did so, the Earth shook.

People in China explained earthquakes by saying that the Great Dragon, who lived deep inside the Earth, shook the ground when annoyed. Japanese earthquakes were said to be caused by sudden movements of the Giant Catfish who carried the world on its back. According to old Russian tales, a giant god traveled through the snow-covered fields by dogsled. The ground shook whenever the dogs scratched at their fleas.

This print shows businessmen punishing the catfish of legend for causing the quake that devastated their city.

Jewish and Christian people of long ago believed that God sent earthquakes to punish the wicked. The sixtieth psalm in the Old Testament reads: "Thou hast made the earth to tremble; thou hast broken it…"

Earthquakes have been studied scientifically for only about 250 years. English scientist John Michell was a pioneer of earthquake studies. In 1760 Michell put us on the right trail by linking earthquakes to massive movements of rocks. Ninety-nine years later, in 1859, Irish scientist Robert Mallet concluded that strain on our planet's crust produced earthquakes. Then, in the 1960s, a new theory about earthquakes was presented. Most scientists now accept this theory.

TECTONIC PLATES

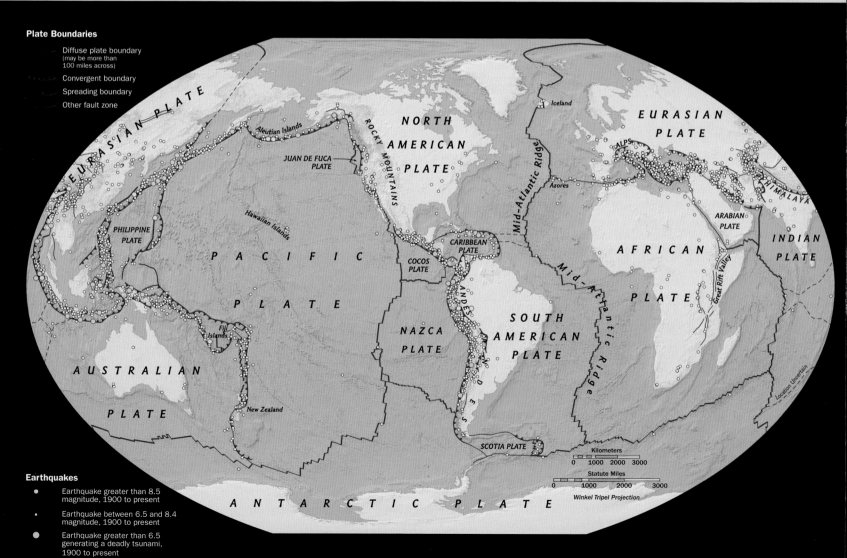

Plate Boundaries

Diffuse plate boundary (may be more than 100 miles across)

Convergent boundary

Spreading boundary

Other fault zone

Earthquakes

● Earthquake greater than 8.5 magnitude, 1900 to present

· Earthquake between 6.5 and 8.4 magnitude, 1900 to present

● Earthquake greater than 6.5 generating a deadly tsunami, 1900 to present

EURASIAN PLATE

Aleutian Islands

JUAN DE FUCA PLATE

ROCKY MOUNTAINS

NORTH AMERICAN PLATE

Iceland

EURASIAN PLATE

ALPS

Azores

Mid-Atlantic Ridge

HIMALAYA

ARABIAN PLATE

INDIAN PLATE

PHILIPPINE PLATE

Hawaiian Islands

PACIFIC PLATE

COCOS PLATE

CARIBBEAN PLATE

AFRICAN PLATE

Great Rift Valley

Mid-Atlantic Ridge

Fiji Islands

NAZCA PLATE

ANDES

SOUTH AMERICAN PLATE

Location Uncertain

AUSTRALIAN PLATE

New Zealand

SCOTIA PLATE

Kilometers
0 1000 2000 3000

Statute Miles
0 1000 2000 3000

Winkel Tripel Projection

ANTARCTIC PLATE

THE PLATE TECTONIC THEORY

Our planet has three basic layers. The outermost layer, called the *crust*, is solid rock. Earth's crust is about 20 miles thick under the continents but is only about 3 miles thick below the oceans. Beneath the crust is Earth's *mantle*, which is composed of hot, solid rock and extends to a depth of 1,800 miles. Earth's innermost layer, the *core*, is our planet's center. Made of both solid and melted metal, the core is extremely hot—up to 13,000 degrees F.

According to the Plate Tectonic Theory, Earth's outer 60-mile-thick shell, including the entire crust and part of the mantle, is composed of a number of separate rocky sections called plates. Our planet has about 14 major and many minor plates.

The plates do not sit still. Pushed by heat currents from deep within the Earth, these large blocks of rock constantly move about—typically half an inch a year. At places where plates meet, they rub against each other, exerting pressure on underground rocks. If the moving plates exert enough pressure on them, the rocks can snap, producing earthquakes. In places where rocks snap easily, small quakes occur. But in other places underground rocks are locked tightly together. The pressure builds until the rocks snap in one giant thrust, producing a massive earthquake.

Places where underground rocks have fractured are called *faults*. As the plates continue to move, they break more rock, causing additional quakes along these faults. The San Andreas is the best-known fault in the United States. Located where the Pacific Plate and the North American Plate meet, the San Andreas Fault extends for 800 miles in California. Many earthquakes have occurred along the San Andreas Fault, including the San Francisco Earthquake of 1906.

> *"In California, the Pacific and North American Plates are sliding past one another along the San Andreas Fault. It's only a matter of time before the edges that are stuck become unstuck."*

Lisa Wald, United States Geological Survey, Earthquake Hazards Program

The movement of the San Andreas Fault

The blue panels in these images represent sea level.

1

2

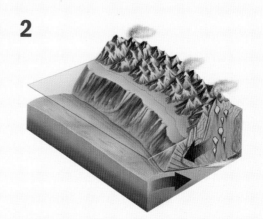

Spreading occurs as tectonic plates beneath the sea slowly move apart from one another. Molten rock from beneath the crust fills the space created by this motion. The molten rock then cools and forms sea-floor mountains. In rare cases, like the East African Rift or Thingvelleir Rift in Iceland (see back cover), these formations can be seen on land.

Powerful earthquakes and volcanic eruptions are caused when the thinner, denser seafloor slips beneath the thicker, lighter continental plates. This process is called subduction. Most of the activity around the Pacific Ring of Fire is the result of subduction.

3

4

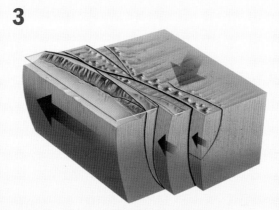

Sometimes, plates slide past one another horizontally, resulting in a vertical fracture in the earth's crust. These are called "strike-slip" faults. The San Andreas is one such fault.

When two plates crush up against one another, land is thrust upward. These plates are said to be converging. This process creates massive earthquakes and spectacular mountains.

Earthquakes aren't the only natural phenomena that occur at plate boundaries. Rocks melt deep underground where the moving plates meet. This molten rock can rise and erupt out of the ground, producing *volcanoes*.

Earth's main earthquake and volcanic zones form patterns that are roughly rectangular or ring-shaped. For example, the Pacific Ring of Fire, a region known for its large number of volcanoes and earthquakes, is located where the Pacific Plate meets other plates.

THE SCIENCE OF SEISMOLOGY

Geologists—scientists who study rocks, mountains, and other aspects of the Earth—include earthquakes in their investigations. There is also a special branch of geology that deals specifically with earthquakes. It is called *seismology*. This name comes from the Greek word *seismos*, meaning "shock" or "earthquake."

Geologists and *seismologists* call the underground location where an earthquake starts the *focus*. They call the place on our planet's surface above the focus the *epicenter*. An earthquake generally is most destructive in the area nearest the epicenter. Since Anchorage wasn't far from the Good Friday Earthquake's epicenter, it suffered catastrophic damage.

Scientists use an instrument called a *seismograph* to detect earthquakes and determine their location and strength. Prince Boris Golitzyn, a Russian seismologist, invented the modern seismograph in the early 1900s.

"The energy produced by an earthquake travels through the ground in the form of what are called *seismic waves*," explains Dr. Roger Hansen, the state seismologist for Alaska. "These waves are what we feel when there's an earthquake."

A quake's strength is called its *magnitude*—abbreviated M. The Richter scale, devised by American seismologist Charles F. Richter in 1935, is often

> **"The ground was quivering like a bowl of jelly... the trees were bending as though they were blowing in a hurricane, but there was not a whisper of wind."**

Doug McRae, recalling the 1964 quake in Alaska

used to measure quakes. "Each whole number on the Richter scale represents a quake about 33 times as powerful as the previous number," continues Dr. Hansen. "This means that an M5.0 earthquake on the Richter scale is 33 times as energetic or powerful as an M4.0 earthquake. An M6.0 quake is about 1,000 times as powerful as an M4.0 quake."

Seismic readings taken in the San Gabriel Mountains and relayed to this seismograph at the California Institute of Technology record an M6.5 earthquake, the San Simeon quake of 2003.

An M2.0 quake on the Richter scale is a minor event. Hundreds of such earthquakes rattle our planet each day without being noticed. Damaging quakes are generally M5.5 or higher. Killer quakes are usually at least M6.0. The most famous quake to strike the United States, the 1906 San Francisco Earthquake, was M8.3, while Alaska's quake that set a North American record in 1964 was M9.2. The most powerful quake ever measured was M9.5. It shook southern Chile in South America in May 1960.

"The magnitude of an earthquake is related to the size of the fault that slipped and how much it slipped, so if you have a bigger fault and more slippage you have a bigger earthquake," explains Lisa Wald, a seismologist with the United States Geological Survey (USGS). "Also, the larger an earthquake's magnitude, the longer it lasts and the more potential damage is involved." A minor quake might last just a second or two. USGS seismologist Dr. Lucy Jones notes, "The San Andreas earthquakes can last one to three minutes. The M9.5 earthquake in Chile was not only

Seismic waves from a 1993 earthquake warped this road on Hokkaido, Japan's northernmost island.

the strongest known quake, it was the quake of the longest duration. It lasted for eleven minutes."

Magnitude isn't the only way to judge a quake's destructive potential. Location is also crucial. Earthquakes in populous areas can cause far more death and destruction than quakes in more remote regions. One reason that China, India, and Japan have suffered some of the deadliest quakes is that these countries have large populations and many big cities.

Some earthquakes are followed by smaller tremors. Called *aftershocks*, they are believed to be caused by smaller breakages of rock following

> *"In a really big earthquake you can actually see seismic waves. During an M7.9 earthquake in southeastern Alaska in 2002, some of my colleagues saw the ground moving like waves move in water. The ground actually rolled as the seismic waves traveled along the surface of the earth."*

Dr. Roger Hansen, seismologist

the big fracture. Aftershocks can bring down buildings that have been badly damaged by the main earthquake. In the aftermath of the Good Friday Earthquake there were more than 7,500 aftershocks.

THE FIVE BIG KILLERS IN EARTHQUAKES

The shaking of the ground is not what kills most victims of earthquakes. A person in an open field would usually be safe during even a gigantic earthquake. Movies about earthquakes often show people disappearing down huge cracks in the earth. This has happened, but it is rare. The main killers in earthquakes are falling buildings, fires, landslides, avalanches, and tsunamis.

When the ground shakes, the vibrations can topple buildings. People both inside and outside can be killed or injured by the falling debris. A 1960 earthquake killed 12,000 people and almost totally destroyed Agadir, Morocco. A survivor commented that Agadir looked "as if a giant foot had stepped on it and squashed it flat."

Earthquakes have set entire cities ablaze. The shaking earth upsets ovens, chimneys, and fireplaces and breaks gas mains (pipes). To make things worse, the quakes can destroy water mains, leaving no way to put out the flames. Fires played such a big role in the famous 1906 disaster that it is sometimes called the Great San Francisco Earthquake and Fire.

Mountainous and hilly regions are the most common sites of earthquakes. The trembling ground can shake dirt, mud, and rocks loose from steep terrain, creating landslides. Snow can also be shaken loose from mountains

On August 17, 1959, two huge earthquakes struck within seconds in Montana, just ten miles northwest of Yellowstone National Park. A mountainside collapsed, sending 80 million tons of rock into the Madison River. The landslide filled the river canyon, creating the 318-foot-deep Earthquake Lake—also known as Quake Lake.

and sent plunging downward in what are called *avalanches*. As the loose materials tumble downhill, landslides and avalanches destroy and bury everything in their path.

Large quakes that strike below or near the ocean sometimes trigger tsunamis. These giant waves can travel thousands of miles, drowning people along seacoasts. In late 2004, a huge earthquake occurred beneath the floor of the Indian Ocean near the Asian country of Indonesia. The giant quake triggered tsunamis that drowned 230,000 people in more than a dozen countries.

CHAPTER 3

"The Heart of This Old Earth Was Broken"

Famous Earthquakes

Six people are dwarfed by the ruins of the Church of Santo Domingo in Arequipa, which was destroyed by the Peru Earthquake of 1868.

Few details are known about some terrible earthquakes of centuries ago. The following aren't necessarily the strongest or the deadliest quakes. However, they are among the most famous because they were well documented.

THE GREAT LISBON EARTHQUAKE OF 1755

November 1, 1755, was All Saints' Day—a Christian holy day. In Lisbon, the capital of Portugal with 250,000 people, churches were lit with candles and filled with morning worshippers.

At 9:30 a.m. a powerful three-minute earthquake rocked Lisbon. After a pause of about 15 minutes, an even stronger five-minute quake struck. Buildings collapsed and fires broke out, claiming thousands of lives.

The earthquake, which seems to have originated on the Atlantic Ocean seabed about 200 miles from Lisbon, also triggered a series of tsunamis. Twenty-foot waves sank ships and drowned thousands of people in Lisbon. Tsunamis created by the Great Lisbon Earthquake also slammed into coastal regions of Spain and Africa and even reached the islands of the West Indies, *4,000 miles* from Lisbon.

Tsunami waves from the Lisbon quake reach the Netherlands, 1,100 miles away.

The shaking earth, fires, and tsunamis claimed at least 60,000 lives and destroyed two-thirds of Lisbon. Due to uncertainties about the number of deaths from the tsunamis, however, the toll may have actually been much higher.

THE NEW MADRID, MISSOURI, EARTHQUAKES OF 1811–1812

At 2:15 a.m. on December 16, 1811, a huge quake jolted New Madrid, Missouri, located on the Mississippi River. Many of the town's one thousand residents fled their shaking cabins and ran outdoors, where the quaking ground tossed them about. Scientists later estimated this quake's magnitude at 8.1, making it the most powerful earthquake ever to strike the nation's midsection. New Madrid resident Eliza Bryan later wrote in a letter:

> *We were visited by a violent shock of an earthquake, accompanied by a very awful noise resembling loud but distant thunder. The screams of the affrighted inhabitants running to and fro, not knowing where to go, or what to do—the cries of the fowls and beasts—the cracking of trees falling, and the roaring of the Mississippi—formed a scene truly horrible.*

Over the next two months many more quakes, a few of them almost as powerful as the first one, shook the New Madrid region. Few buildings within 250 miles of New Madrid remained intact. The quakes reshaped the land. In places the ground was lifted. In other places it sank. Water filled the sunken areas, creating swamps and lakes, including Reelfoot Lake in northwest Tennessee. The town of New Madrid was among the places covered by water. It was later rebuilt more than a mile from its former location, which now lies beneath the Mississippi River.

"The earth waved like a field of corn before the breeze."

Wildlife artist John James Audubon, describing a New Madrid Earthquake he experienced in Kentucky

The quakes also uprooted forests, triggered landslides, and shook bluffs into the Mississippi River. More quakes just a few months later, on February 7, 1812, temporarily changed the contours of the Mississippi River's bed. As a result, portions of the mighty river flowed *backward* for several hours.

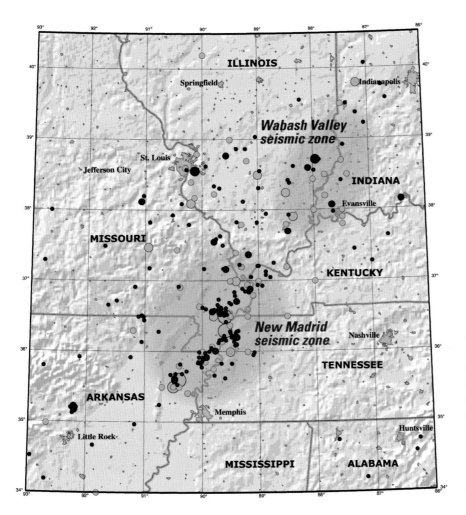

The small circles on this map indicate where earthquakes larger than magnitude 2.5 occurred in the New Madrid and Wabash Valley seismic zones. The red circles show where such quakes occurred between 1974 and 2002; the green circles denote earlier earthquakes. Bigger circles represent larger tremors.

For many years, the New Madrid Earthquakes were considered oddities. They had not occurred in a mountainous region. They had not taken place at the edges of tectonic plates, but in the middle of the North American Plate. It seemed unlikely that another major earthquake could rock the middle of the country again.

Then, in the 1970s, geologists discovered that faults dating from hundreds of millions of years ago lie beneath the ground in the New Madrid region. The slow movement of the North American Plate can break rocks along these faults, producing quakes as strong as those at plate boundaries. The bottom line is that mid-America could have more quakes as powerful as the New Madrid Earthquakes of 1811–1812. The difference is that the region is now highly populated, with such large cities as St. Louis, Missouri; Memphis and Nashville, Tennessee; and Little Rock, Arkansas. A repeat of the New Madrid Earthquakes of two centuries ago would be catastrophic today.

THE GREAT SAN FRANCISCO EARTHQUAKE AND FIRE OF 1906

Founded in 1776, San Francisco remained a small town until gold was discovered in California in 1848. As the gold miners' supply station, San Francisco became a boom town. By 1906 it was one of the nation's major cities with a half-million people.

Its location near several of California's many faults, including the San Andreas Fault, made San Francisco prone to earthquakes. Quakes shook the region in 1838 and 1868. But no one was prepared for what happened in the spring of 1906.

At 5:12 a.m. on April 18, underground rocks broke along the San Andreas Fault just ten miles from San Francisco. A loud roar could be heard as the earth shook for a minute, toppling buildings.

"Did you ever see a dog shake a rat?" survivor Warren Olney later wrote. "We were like rats in a dog's mouth. Old Mother Earth appeared to be trying to shake us off her face." A policeman who was on patrol at the time of the quake

reported that "'The ground seemed to twist under us like a top while it jerked this way and that, and up and down and every way.'"

Within 15 minutes, dozens of fires were raging in downtown San Francisco. The fires burned for three days and were so intense that reddish smoke was visible to ships 100 miles out at sea.

The quake and fires destroyed much of San Francisco. Half the city's residents lost their homes. Many survivors fled San Francisco and never returned, making an accurate casualty count impossible. Although the death toll from the Great San Francisco Earthquake and Fire is often placed at 700, some historians insist that more than 3,000 people died in this disaster.

JAPAN'S GREAT EARTHQUAKE OF 1923

Because it is located on the edge of the Eurasian Plate near its boundary with the Pacific Plate, Japan has been struck by many earthquakes. The country has even been called the world's earthquake factory. On September 1, 1923, at two minutes before noon, a tremendous quake shook Japan's Sagami Bay region, near the cities of Tokyo and Yokohama.

Many people in Japan had been cooking their noontime meal when the earthquake struck. As buildings in Tokyo and Yokohama toppled, stoves overturned. Fires ignited and grew so large that they generated their own

Survivors of the 1923 Earthquake gather in Tokyo's Euno Park as their city burns.

winds, creating what are called *firestorms*. In Tokyo, more than 40,000 people sought safety in an open park known as the Military Clothing Depot. Nearby buildings caught fire, launching a firestorm that swept through the crowd like a flaming hurricane at 150 miles per hour. At that one location, at least 38,000 people perished.

To make the disaster even worse, the quake caused the ground in the Sagami Bay region to rise in some places and fall in others. The movement of land in the area of the bay triggered 30-foot tsunamis that flooded Japanese cities and towns.

Fires, toppling buildings, and tsunamis claimed up to 150,000 lives. Roughly half of Tokyo and most of Yokohama were destroyed by the Great Earthquake of 1923. Because of extensive damage to Tokyo's telephone and telegraph wires, the city turned to an unusual means of communication. For a week after the earthquake, messages were sent out of Tokyo by 400 specially trained carrier pigeons.

PERU'S EARTHQUAKE, AVALANCHES, AND LANDSLIDES OF 1970

At 3:23 p.m., on May 31, 1970, an earthquake jolted the South American country of Peru. Enormous damage occurred in Peru's coastal department of Ancash. (Departments in Peru are similar to states in the United States.) In the city of Huaraz, as many as 20,000 people died in the crumbling buildings. Chimbote and other towns in the area were also greatly damaged or destroyed.

The quake's focus was 15 miles off the coast of Peru, far below the Pacific Ocean seafloor. Due to the great depth of its point of origin, the quake did not disturb the seabed, so no major tsunamis occurred. But while it produced no killers from the ocean depths, the quake triggered some deadly events from the heights of Peru.

WITNESS TO A LANDSLIDE

"I heard a great roar coming from Huascaran. It looked as though a large mass of rock and ice was breaking loose. My immediate reaction was to run for the high ground of Cemetery Hill, situated about 150 to 200 meters away. I reached the upper level of the cemetery near the top just as the debris flow struck the base of the hill and I was probably only 10 seconds ahead of it.

"At about the same time, I saw a man just a few meters down the hill who was carrying two small children.

"The debris flow caught him and he threw the two children towards the hilltop to safety, although the debris flow swept him down the valley, never to be seen again."

Mateo Casaverde, a Peruvian scientist who was in the city of Yungay when the Huascaran avalanche-landslide struck.

An M7.6 quake in San Salvador sparked this devastating landslide.

The quake shook loose a huge mass of material from Huascaran, the 22,205-foot mountain that is Peru's highest peak, unleashing a combination avalanche-landslide. Millions of tons of snow, ice, rocks, and mud shot down the mountain's slopes at speeds sometimes exceeding 150 miles per hour. In Yungay, 20,000 people were buried alive. Elsewhere the half-mile-wide mass of debris flattened villages and farms like a giant bulldozer. When it finally ended, the Peruvian quake and accompanying landslide-avalanche had claimed nearly 80,000 lives and had destroyed the homes of nearly a million people. It was the deadliest natural disaster ever to strike North or South America.

CHINA'S GREAT QUAKE OF 1976

China, the world's most populous country, has suffered some of the greatest natural disasters, including floods, famines, and earthquakes. The deadliest known quake in history shook China in 1556, taking about 830,000 lives. Four hundred twenty years later, on the morning of July 28, 1976, China was rocked by a quake that was almost as deadly.

Witnesses later recalled that, in the hours before the giant quake, flashes of light illuminated the sky. Known as earthquake lights (EQLs for short), this phenomenon has occasionally been observed prior to quakes, although their cause remains a mystery. Then, at 3:42 a.m., millions of people in northeastern China's Hopeh Province were awakened by a loud roar. An M8.2 earthquake shook the ground violently on that rainy Wednesday morning. The quake's epicenter was in a highly populated area: Tangshan, a coal-mining city with about a million residents.

Buildings crumbled so quickly they appeared to be "made of cards," a survivor later reported. Another explained that when the earthquake struck she thought the building she was in "had been hit by a nuclear bomb." Coal tunnels beneath Tangshan collapsed, burying miners working the night shift. Pits created by the collapsing mines swallowed up a train and a hospital.

Few photographs exist of earthquake lights, although people have reported seeing them before and after major quakes. Scientists are studying them as possible earthquake predictors. This photograph was taken in China.

Beijing, the capital of China, and Tianjin, another major Chinese city, were also damaged by the quake. Across the nearby countryside, dams collapsed, railroad tracks were wrecked, and trees were uprooted.

Just 15 hours following the first earthquake, another major quake struck. Fortunately, most people who had survived the first quake were camping in fields and on streets, where they were safe from further building collapses.

It is believed that 750,000 people died in China's Great Quake of July 28, 1976. As with any disaster of this magnitude, it is difficult to know the true number of casualties.

"Only a Matter of Time"
Predicting and Preparing for Earthquakes

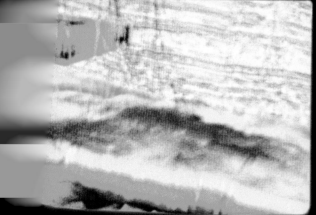
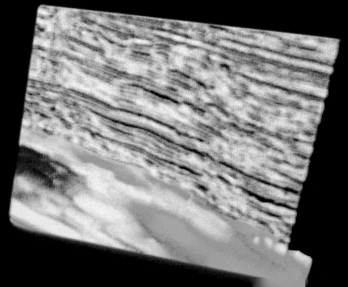

Geologists use special 3-D glasses to view layers of rock beneath the Earth. The images are generated by probes which use bursts of energy to create mini-earthquakes. The different colors show various rock formations.

Survivors of a December 2005 quake in Pakistan use a damaged bridge to get supplies.

If we knew when and where earthquakes were coming, thousands of lives could be spared. Seismologists have correctly predicted some quakes in the United States, Greece, and other countries. Their greatest triumph happened in China in 1975. Early that February, Chinese scientists predicted that a giant quake was about to rock Liaoning Province in the northeastern part of the country. Radio warnings were broadcast urging people to leave their homes and take refuge in open places. Nearly everyone followed the advice. As predicted, a huge quake shook Liaoning Province on February 4, damaging or destroying almost every building in the city of Haicheng. Had there been no warning, an estimated half-million people might have died. But there *was* a warning, and few people perished.

> **"...equivalent to all the world's nuclear arsenals unleashed on the sea floor at once."**
>
> **Dr. Hermann M. Fritz** on the power of a M9.3 Indian Ocean earthquake

Seismologists have several tools to help them predict quakes. One of the most valuable is the seismograph, the instrument used to detect earthquakes. Roughly half of all earthquakes are preceded by smaller quakes, known as *foreshocks*. If seismographs record a number of small quakes in an area, it may be a clue that a much larger quake is about to occur.

Although most faults are concealed within the Earth, some, including California's San Andreas Fault, are partly visible at the Earth's surface. Seismologists place *strainmeters* across faults to measure rock movement along these fractures in the ground. When strainmeters indicate that rocks along a fault are under severe stress, it may mean that the rocks will soon break and cause an earthquake.

Another instrument, the *tiltmeter*, can detect small changes in the tilt or slope of the ground. Changes in tilt along a fault may mean that underground rocks are shifting and could soon break.

Our planet itself seems to send out hints that earthquakes are about to occur. The Earth produces electric signals. Some scientists have made successful predictions based on changes that occur in these natural electric signals prior to quakes. Magnetic and gravitational changes may also occur in the ground before earthquakes occur.

Water in wells can provide clues that earthquakes are about to strike. Because shifting rocks change the pressure on liquids, a well's water level may change before a quake. Rocks that are breaking underground can add particles of earth to well water, causing it to turn muddy. The amount of *radon gas*, a radioactive element, often increases in well water prior to a quake.

Animals seem to sense when earthquakes are coming. There have been hundreds of reports of dogs, cats, birds, cockroaches, and rats becoming disturbed and disoriented prior to quakes. The night before the 1906 quake, horses in San Francisco grew panicky. The day before the 1964 Good Friday Earthquake, Alaska's Kodiak bears came out of hibernation weeks ahead of schedule.

An assortment of clues alerted scientists that a big quake was about to strike China in 1975. Seismographs detected numerous foreshocks in the days before the giant quake. Well water turned muddy and revealed an increase in radon gas. The ground exhibited changes in tilt as well as

A scientist on Mount St. Helens, Washington, installs a Global Positioning System (GPS). In September of 2004 an earthquake swarm of M2.5 and larger quakes occurred once a minute. The volcanic Mount Adams is in the distance.

electrical and magnetic variations. Farm animals and pets acted strangely. Taken all together, these clues convinced scientists that the ground was about to shake, and this is what happened when the big quake struck Liaoning Province. Just the next year, however, China's Hopeh Province Earthquake caught almost everyone by surprise. Three quarters of a million people died.

"No one knows if we ever will be able to consistently predict earthquakes," says seismologist Lisa Wald. "Earthquakes in different places are all different. Clues involving well water and strange animal behavior don't predict earthquakes consistently. Sometimes they occur and there's no earthquake. Sometimes they don't happen and there is a quake."

Some of the best warnings—when they occur—are foreshocks. Yet foreshocks can't serve as consistent clues, either. "Only about half of our big damaging earthquakes are preceded by these smaller earthquakes," says Dr. Lucy Jones. Also, in many cases it is difficult to tell whether smaller earthquakes are foreshocks or whether they're all that's going to happen.

Researchers continue to seek new ways to improve earthquake prediction. For example, some scientists in China are studying snakes in the belief that they exhibit unusual behavior up to five days prior to earthquakes. But, Lisa Wald points out, "perhaps more important than predicting quakes is to be able to survive and withstand them. To do that, we must prepare for them."

MINIMIZING DEATH AND DESTRUCTION FROM EARTHQUAKES

In 1946, an Alaskan quake launched giant waves that killed 159 people in Hawaii, some 2,300 miles away. The United States then established a Pacific Ocean tsunami warning system headquartered in Hawaii. The disastrous earthquake and tsunamis in 1964 led to the development of a warning center in Palmer, Alaska. Both centers rely on earthquake monitoring stations around the world as well as dozens of wave-watching stations in the Pacific Ocean. Within a half hour of a quake, the centers can send out *tsunami watches*, indicating that tsunamis may occur.

If an actual tsunami is detected, the centers issue *tsunami warnings* indicating when and where a huge wave may strike. By warning people of approaching tsunamis along the coastal regions of the United States, around the Pacific Rim, and in the Caribbean area, the systems may save thousands of lives in years to come.

There are other ways to minimize the death and destruction from earthquakes. Seismologists say, "Earthquakes don't kill people; buildings kill people." In regions that are prone to quakes, it is crucial to construct homes and other buildings out of the most quake-resistant materials available.

Crew members aboard the National Oceanic and Atmospheric Association (NOAA) floating scientific laboratory deploy one of the tsunami buoys that measure rises in the level of the ocean. Such buoys alert the Pacific Tsunami Warning Center when an earthquake triggers a tsunami wave.

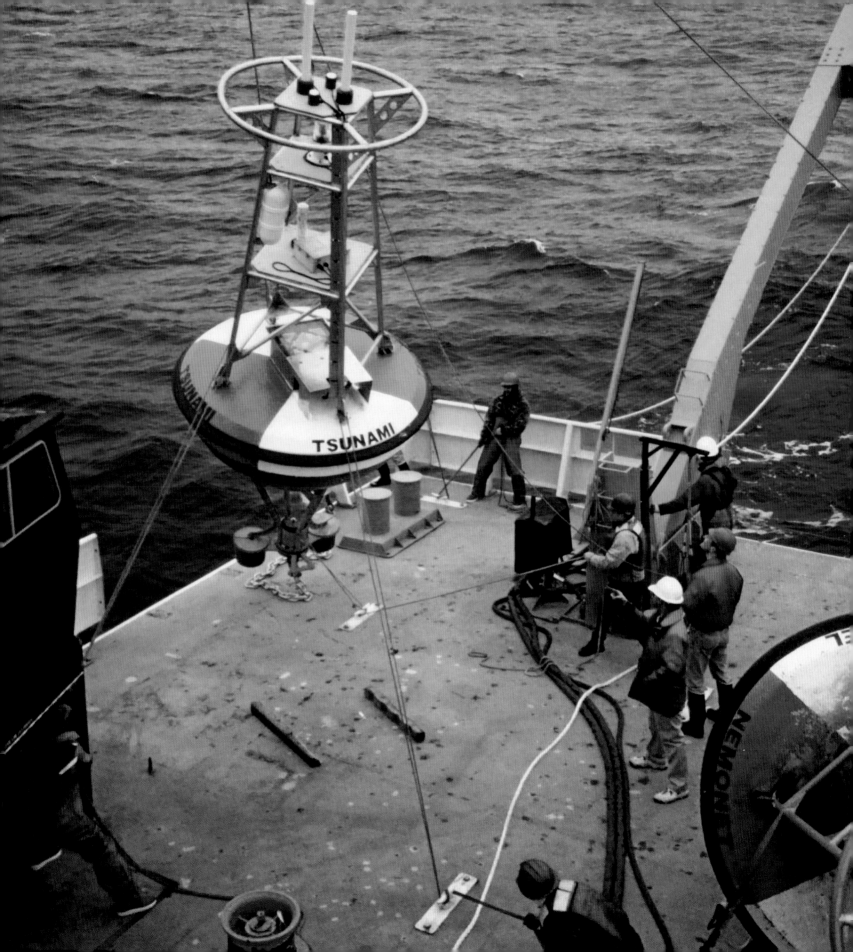

"We were driving on the Bay Bridge's lower level chatting about the Goodyear Blimp that was hovering over Candlestick Park when the bridge began to sway," recalled **Ray Ungson.** *"The top part of the bridge fell down. A big section fell to our level five or six cars ahead of us. People were in a panic—climbing out of car windows, crying, and praying. We didn't know what was going to fall next. From the bridge, we could see that part of San Francisco was in flames."* At the time of the quake **Captain John Crayton** was piloting that blimp 1,000 feet above Candlestick Park in preparation for the World Series game. *"We saw what looked like puffs of smoke coming from a small hill just west of the ballpark. At first, we thought it was just a rock slide. Then we saw numerous transformers blowing up below us. When the sun set, the city went pitch black.... . Ours were the first—and only—pictures from the air. We expected to be airborne for 3½ hours televising the World Series game. Instead, we spent the next 13 hours covering the earthquake's aftermath."*

Ray Ungson was carpooling home from work when the Loma Prieta Earthquake struck at 5:04 p.m. on October 17, 1989. The Goodyear Blimp's television coverage made it possible for police, firefighters, and other emergency personnel in Oakland and San Francisco to coordinate their postearthquake rescue efforts. **Captain Crayton** again piloted the airship after the 1989 World Series—also called the Earthquake Series—resumed.

This damaged section of the Bay Bridge near Oakland, California, is about 60 miles from the quake's epicenter in the Santa Cruz Mountains.

Rescue workers and their dogs search for victims in the rubble of a collapsed department store in a Santa Cruz, California, shopping mall after the 1989 Loma Prieta Earthquake. Santa Cruz lies about ten miles from the earthquake's epicenter.

For example, steel, reinforced concrete, and wood are good building materials, because they can flex somewhat without breaking. Family homes built completely out of brick are not as safe, because they can break apart easily. Tall buildings should be anchored in solid rock. Buildings should also have substantial foundations. Dangerous places to build include steep slopes, bluffs, and other places subject to landslides.

Says Dr. Jones, "The biggest thing we've done in the United States to protect people from earthquakes is that we've established building codes. We have legislation not allowing people to construct the kind of buildings that tend to fall down where there are big earthquakes."

As long as there is an Earth, there will be earthquakes. But by preparing for them—and by learning more about when and where they are likely to strike—we can limit the harm from these violent acts of nature.

The December 26, 2003, earthquake in Bam, Iran, killed more than 26,000 people and left 60,000 homeless during freezing weather. The massive quake occurred at 5:28 a.m., when most victims were asleep in homes that collapsed. This framed photograph was buried under the rubble of one such house.

"Civilization exists by geological consent, subject to change without notice."

Historian Will Durant

Glossary

aftershocks—smaller quakes that can follow major quakes as broken underground rocks settle

avalanche—fast-moving slide of snow down mountain slopes

core—the Earth's innermost layer or center

crust—the outside layer of the Earth

earthquake—a shaking of the ground caused by the breaking of underground rocks

epicenter—the place on our planet's surface directly above the focus of an earthquake

fault—place where underground rocks have broken

firestorm—a fire that creates its own strong winds

focus—the underground place where an earthquake starts

foreshock—smaller quake that precedes some major quakes

geologist—a scientist who studies rocks, mountains, and other aspects of the Earth

landslide—fast-moving slide of dirt, mud, and rocks down mountain slopes

Instead of taking his usual train, this man follows the tracks after a quake in Kobe, Japan.

magnitude—a quake's strength or the amount of energy it releases

mantle—the layer of planet Earth beneath the crust and above the core

Plate Tectonic Theory—the scientific idea that the Earth's crust and mantle are composed of a number of rigid, rocky, slowly moving plates, or segments

radon gas—a radioactive gas that often increases in the Earth's crust in places where earthquakes are about to occur

seismic wave—the vibration from earthquakes that travels through the Earth; they are what we feel when there is an earthquake

seismograph—*an instrument that detects and measures earthquakes*

seismologist—*earthquake expert*

seismology—*a branch of geology that deals specifically with earthquakes*

strainmeter—*instrument that measures rock movements along faults*

tiltmeter—*an instrument that measures changes in the tilt or slope of the ground*

tsunami—*huge sea wave created by earthquakes or volcanic eruptions beneath or near the sea*

volcano—*the opening in the ground through which hot rock erupts; the mountain that such eruptions create*

A car is crushed beneath a building that collapsed during an earthquake in western Turkey.

Bibliography

BOOKS

After the Tangshan Earthquake: How the Chinese People Overcame a Major Natural Disaster. Peking: Foreign Languages Press, 1976.

Davison, Charles. *The Japanese Earthquake of 1923.* London: Thomas Murby, 1931.

Engle, Eloise. *Earthquake! The Story of Alaska's Good Friday Disaster.* New York: John Day, 1966.

Fradkin, Philip L. *The Great Earthquake and Firestorms of 1906: How San Francisco Nearly Destroyed Itself.* Berkeley: University of California Press, 2005.

Hough, Susan Elizabeth. *Earthshaking Science: What We Know (and Don't Know) about Earthquakes.* Princeton, N.J.: Princeton University Press, 2002.

National Research Council, Committee on the Alaska Earthquake. *The Great Alaska Earthquake of 1964: Biology.* Washington, D.C.: National Academy of Sciences, 1971.

National Research Council, Committee on the Alaska Earthquake. *The Great Alaska Earthquake of 1964: Human Ecology.* Washington, D.C.: National Academy of Sciences, 1970.

Tazieff, Haroun. *Earthquake Prediction.* New York: McGraw-Hill, 1992.

U.S. Coast and Geodetic Survey. *The Prince William Sound, Alaska, Earthquake of 1964 and Aftershocks (vols. I, II-A, II-BC, and III).* Washington, D.C.: United States Government Printing Office, 1966–1969.

Zeilinga de Boer, Jelle, and Donald Theodore Sanders. *Earthquakes in Human History: The Far-Reaching Effects of Seismic Disruptions.* Princeton, N.J.: Princeton University Press, 2005.

Zongjin, Ma, Fu Zhengxiang, Zhang Yingzhen, Wang Chengmin, Zhang Guomin, and Liu Defu. *Earthquake Prediction: Nine Major Earthquakes in China (1966–1976).* Beijing: Seismological Press, 1990.

In 1964, the newly constructed Showa Bridge in Japan did not withstand its first earthquake.

Further Reading and Research

FOR FURTHER READING

Claybourne, Anna. *Read About Earthquakes.* Brookfield, Conn.: Copper Beech Books, 2000.

Gentle, Victor, and Janet Perry. *Earthquakes.* Milwaukee: Gareth Stevens, 2001.

Lassieur, Allison. *Earthquakes.* Mankato, Minn.: Capstone Press, 2001.

Nicolson, Cynthia Pratt. *Earthquake!* Tonawanda, N.Y.: Kids Can Press, 2002.

Reed, Jennifer. *Earthquakes: Disaster & Survival.* Berkeley Heights, N.J.: Enslow, 2005.

Richards, Julie. *Quivering Quakes.* Broomall, Penn.: Chelsea House, 2002.

Tanaka, Shelley. *Earthquake! On a Peaceful Spring Morning, Disaster Strikes San Francisco.* New York: Hyperion Books for Children, 2004.

Thoron, Joe. *Earthquakes.* Tarrytown, N.Y.: Marshall Cavendish Benchmark, 2007.

WEBSITES TO EXPLORE

For useful information from the USGS on such topics as where and how earthquakes occur, and measuring and predicting earthquakes:

http://pubs.usgs.gov/gip/earthq1/

For a wealth of information for kids on earthquakes from the USGS:

http://earthquake.usgs.gov/learning/kids.php

For basic information on earthquakes, including information on plate tectonics and earthquake safety tips:

http://www.weatherwizkids.com/earthquake1.htm

A website about earthquakes for young people that includes earthquake legends from around the world:

http://www.fema.gov/kids/quake.htm

A short description of some notable earthquakes, mostly from the 20th century:

http://www.pdc.org/iweb/earthquake_history.jsp

Interviews by the Authors

SCIENTISTS

Delores Clark, NOAA Public Affairs Officer, Honolulu, Hawaii

Dr. Hermann M. Fritz, School of Civil and Environmental Engineering, Georgia Institute of Technology

Dr. Roger Hansen, state seismologist and professor of seismology, Geophysical Institute, University of Alaska-Fairbanks

Dr. Lucy Jones, seismologist, United States Geological Survey, Pasadena, California

Dr. Alberto M. Lopez-Venegas, Woods Hole Science Center, Eastern Region, United States Geological Survey

Lisa Wald, seismologist, United States Geological Survey, Golden, Colorado

WITNESSES TO EARTHQUAKES

Geraldina Alfano

Vito Alfano

Laura Barton

Captain John Crayton

Mollie Doran Crittenden

Michele Doran

Susan Doran

Vincent Doran

V. J. Doran

John Eads

Robert Eads

Nedeljko Kalabic

Zrinka Kalabic

Linda McRae MacSwain

Susan Martinson

Doug McRae

Ray Ungson

Viola Simeonoff-Inga

Acknowledgments

A special "thank you" to **Joy Ikelman** of the National Geophysical Data Center for providing beautiful pictures for this as well as our other Witness to Disaster books.

About Our Experts

"I was born in San Antonio, Texas, but I always wanted to live in Colorado, where I began collecting rocks while on vacations. Science has always interested me, but choosing a specialty was not easy. I wandered from biology to pre-med and finally into geology with a specialty in earthquake seismology. I felt my first earthquake three months after I got my job with the USGS in Pasadena, California, in 1987. After 20 years in California, I transferred to the Colorado office, where I manage the website for the USGS Earthquake Hazards Program, with a focus on education and real-time earthquake information. I live in Evergreen, Colorado, with my husband, who is also a seismologist, two children, and two kitties."

—**Lisa Wald,** USGS

"I was fortunate to be born and grow up on the lovely tropical island of Puerto Rico. Learning how our planet was formed and what it has gone through over time inspired me to study geology at the University of Puerto Rico–Mayaguez Campus. I obtained my doctoral degree from Northwestern University in Evanston, Illinois, where I studied earthquakes. I now live in Woods Hole, Massachusetts, where I have been working with the USGS on how earthquakes can trigger tsunamis. I hope to apply all that I have learned to help people understand and be aware of the effects of earthquakes."

—**Dr. Alberto M. Lopez-Venegas,** USGS

If you have a question about earthquakes, or if you want to talk about earthquakes, feel free to contact the authors. Dennis and Judy can be reached at: fradinbooks@comcast.net

Index